Big Cats

Tiger

Written by
Tom Riddolls

www.av2books.com

AV² provides enriched content that supplements and complements this book. Weigl's AV² books strive to create inspired learning and engage young minds in a total learning experience.

Your AV² Media Enhanced books come alive with...

Audio
Listen to sections of the book read aloud.

Video
Watch informative video clips.

Embedded Weblinks
Gain additional information for research.

Try This!
Complete activities and hands-on experiments.

Key Words
Study vocabulary, and complete a matching word activity.

Quizzes
Test your knowledge.

Slide Show
View images and captions, and prepare a presentation.

... and much, much more!

Go to **www.av2books.com,** and enter this book's unique code.

BOOK CODE

X339015

AV² by Weigl brings you media enhanced books that support active learning.

Published by AV² by Weigl
350 5ᵗʰ Avenue, 59ᵗʰ Floor
New York, NY 10118
Websites: www.av2books.com   www.weigl.com

Library of Congress Cataloging-in-Publication Data

Riddolls, Tom, author.
 Tiger / Tom Riddolls.
    pages cm. -- (Big cats)
 Includes index.
 ISBN 978-1-4896-0930-4 (hardcover : alk. paper) -- ISBN 978-1-4896-0931-1 (softcover : alk. paper) -- ISBN 978-1-4896-0932-8 (single user ebk.) -- ISBN 978-1-4896-0933-5 (multi user ebk.)
 1. Tiger--Juvenile literature. I. Title.
 QL737.C23R535 2015
 599.756--dc23

2014004318

Printed in the United States of America in North Mankato, Minnesota
1 2 3 4 5 6 7 8 9 0 18 17 16 15 14

032014
WEP150314

Editor Heather Kissock   Design Terry Paulhus

Contents

Meet the Tiger

Tigers are part of the cat **family**. They are the largest type of cat in the world. Tigers like to hunt big animals such as deer and wild pigs. An animal that hunts other animals for food is a predator. Tigers do not hunt in groups. In fact, they spend most of their lives alone. Animals that live that way are **solitary**.

In nature, tigers live only in Asia. Each tiger claims a **territory** as its own. Tigers mark this area with their scent. Scientists have found that tigers can recall things very well. They do not forget as easily as other types of creatures. This helps them to guard their territories.

Unlike most big cats, tigers love to swim. The jaguar is the only other big cat that shares the tiger's fondness of the water.

All About Tigers

The tiger is best known for its stripes. Tigers are the only big cats that have striped coats. Their coats are mostly orange, with black or dark brown stripes.

Tigers range in size depending on the **subspecies**. The size of a particular tiger also depends on whether it is male or female. In general, adult male tigers are larger than adult female tigers.

The largest tiger subspecies is the Siberian tiger. Adult males of this subspecies can weigh up to 675 pounds (306 kg) and grow to be 10.8 feet (3.3 m) long. The smallest living subspecies is the Sumatran tiger. Adult male Sumatran tigers weigh up to 309 pounds (140 kg) and can be up to 8.4 feet (2.6 m) in length.

Like other large cats, tigers use roars to communicate over long distances. However, tigers cannot purr.

Comparing Big Cats

The tiger is very fast for its size. The leopard and cheetah are faster but cannot kill as big an animal as the tiger can. Some tigers can eat up to 80 pounds (36.24 kg) of meat in a day. They need large **prey** to support their diet.

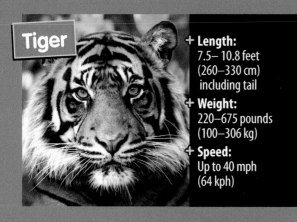

Tiger

+ **Length:**
7.5– 10.8 feet (260–330 cm) including tail
+ **Weight:**
220–675 pounds (100–306 kg)
+ **Speed:**
Up to 40 mph (64 kph)

Lion

+ **Length:**
6.5–9 feet (198–274 cm) including tail
+ **Weight:**
265–420 lbs (120–190 kg)
+ **Speed:**
Up to 35 mph (56 kph)

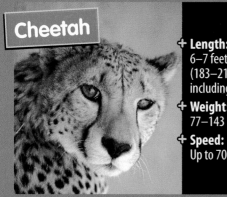

Cheetah

+ **Length:**
6–7 feet (183–213 cm) including tail
+ **Weight:**
77–143 lbs (35–65 kg)
+ **Speed:**
Up to 70 mph (112 kph)

Leopard

+ **Length:**
6.5–9 feet (198–274 cm) including tail
+ **Weight:**
66–176 lbs (30–80 kg)
+ **Speed:**
Up to 57 mph (92 kph)

Jaguar

+ **Length:**
7–9 feet (213–274 cm) including tail
+ **Weight:**
100–250 lbs (45–113 kg)
+ **Speed:**
Up to 40 mph (64 kph)

Cougar

+ **Length:**
5–9 feet (152–274 cm) including tail
+ **Weight:**
Up to 150 lbs (68 kg)
+ **Speed:**
Up to 35 mph (56 kph)

Tiger History

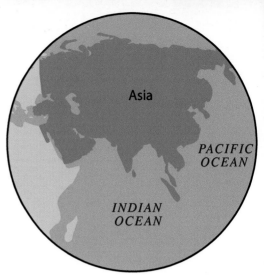

Asia

PACIFIC OCEAN

INDIAN OCEAN

The first tigers appeared on Earth 2 million years ago. They came from the same **ancestor** as the other big cats. Tigers are part of the **genus** Panthera. The word *Panthera* means "big spotted cat." The genus Panthera includes tigers, lions, leopards, and jaguars.

Panthera **evolved** about 10.8 million years ago. The first cats lived in Asia. While other big cats moved as far away as Africa and the Americas, tigers stayed in Asia. Some tigers went north into Russia. Some went south to the Indonesian islands.

The number of tigers has dropped recently. In 1900, there were more than 100,000 tigers. Today, there are fewer than 4,000. People cut down parts of jungles to build cities and plant crops. This means tigers have lost those places to live. Tigers now have less than one tenth of the land they used to have.

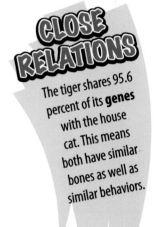

CLOSE RELATIONS

The tiger shares 95.6 percent of its **genes** with the house cat. This means both have similar bones as well as similar behaviors.

Siberian tigers are now called Amur tigers. They no longer live in Siberia, but they are found in the Amur Valley in Russia.

Where Tigers Live

Tigers can be found in a variety of **habitats**. Some tigers live in snowy, mountainous areas. Others live in hot jungles.

Tigers' territories can vary widely. Some areas can be more than 620 square miles (997.7 sq. km). Others can be one tenth of that size. Females usually have smaller territories than males.

Tigers choose their territory because the area has what they need to survive. They often choose areas with tall grass. This helps them hide when hunting. Tigers also choose territories that have many prey animals. Tigers often make several **dens** around their territory where they can rest in safety.

Tigers live in isolated pockets of land. There are rarely more than 12 tigers in any one area.

KEEP THEIR COOL

Tigers that live in hot jungles often stay cool by lying in water.

Tiger Features

Tigers are **adapted** for hunting large animals in tall grass. Their heavy bodies and large paws are good for catching prey. Tigers use their stripes to blend in with their surroundings. This helps them sneak close to prey before attacking.

2

4

Getting Closer

① Teeth

- Used to grab prey and tear meat
- Can be up to 5 inches (13 cm) long

② Coat

- Usually orange fur with stripes
- White patches above eyes, on stomachs, and on mouths
- Black ears with one large white spot

③ Throat

- Talks to other tigers by roaring
- Roar possible due to structure of throat
- Does not roar to scare away danger

④ Hind Legs

- Back legs built to leap on prey
- Can jump more than 33 feet (10 meters)

⑤ Paws

- Large and softly-padded paws
- Claws up to 5 inches (13 cm)
- Uses claws to hold onto prey

What Do Tigers Eat?

Tigers must eat a large amount of food because of their hefty size. To get enough to eat, tigers hunt animals that will feed them for several days. These animals include wild pigs, buffalo, and deer. Some tigers also eat crocodiles and even young elephants.

Most tigers eat about 20 pounds (9 kg) of meat at a time. They eat three or four times a day. Tigers bury their food under leaves and stay close to it until they have finished eating. Often, they wait a few days before hunting again. Tigers must eat regularly, though. They will starve to death in two weeks if they do not eat.

Tigers are known to be a key predator of the Malayan tapir. This animal can weigh up to 900 pounds (405 kilograms).

ENOUGH TO SHARE

Tigers will sometimes share their food. This sharing ensures that sick or injured tigers get to eat as well.

Tiger
Life Cycle

Adult tigers live alone except when mating. The female tiger can only mate for five days each year. The scent she leaves on the ground attracts the closest male. The female tiger will also make special cries that announce she is ready to mate. The male tiger has to be careful after he mates with the female. Female tigers often try to hurt males after mating.

Birth to 2 Weeks

Tiger cubs are born with their eyes closed. They open their eyes after a week. However, they cannot see properly for several weeks. Cubs are born with the same strip pattern they will have as adults. At birth, most cubs weigh 3 pounds (1.4 kg).

Tigers give birth about 100 days after mating. Their litters often have three babies, called cubs. The young tigers will not leave their mother until they are 2 years old.

2 Years and Older

It takes five years for a tiger to reach full size. During this time, the tiger will move around looking for its own territory. Unlike females, males will often move very far from their mothers. Only half of the cubs born will grow to be adults. In nature, tigers often live 15 years. In zoos, tigers can get much older. Some live about 25 years.

2 Weeks to 2 Years

For the first six months, tiger cubs live off their mother's milk. After this, they begin to eat only what their mother kills. Cubs spend most of their first two years playing and learning to hunt. At two years, the mother forces them to leave so she can mate again.

Conservation of Tigers

Since 1940, people have hunted three kinds of tigers to **extinction**. The Bali, Caspian, and Javan tigers can no longer be found living anywhere on Earth. Tigers are killed for a variety of reasons. Some people kill tigers because they fear them. Others hunt them because tigers hurt farm animals. Still others kill tigers to sell the tigers' body parts.

Human activity, such as clearing land for farms, also drives away prey animals. Many tigers now live and hunt in protected areas, where there are guards to keep **poachers** out. In India, a program called Project Tiger keeps tigers safe in 27 special parks. The group runs tiger reserves where the numbers of tigers are growing instead of decreasing.

IN DANGER

Tiger are one of the top 10 most endangered animals on the planet. Tiger skins are sometimes made into rugs. These can sell for thousands of dollars.

Efforts to preserve tiger populations have led to increased anti-poaching measures throughout India.

DONATED BY
GLOBAL TIGER PATROL

Myths and Legends

People in Asian countries have many legends about tigers. Some people think tigers are evil. Others think they are gods that keep humans safe. In Chinese mythology, tigers stand for the physical world. They have marks on their heads that some people think look like the Mandarin word *wang*. *Wang* means "king," so many Chinese people call the tiger the "King of Animals."

In Korea, some people feel that tigers keep away bad spirits. They hang pictures of tigers in their houses. They believe the pictures will scare the spirits away. Some Koreans feel that wearing tiger claws and bones will keep them safe. To them, tiger jewelry brings good luck.

During India's Onam festival, people paint their bodies like tigers. They perform a dance that tells the story of a tiger hunt.

Hiding in Plain Sight

Many animals use camouflage. The colors and shapes of their bodies help them blend in with their surroundings. A tiger's camouflage helps to keep it hidden in its jungle home. To see how a tiger uses camouflage, try this activity.

Materials Needed: You will need four or five sheets of paper, scissors, tape, and markers.

STEP 1 Make two jungle scenes on large sheets of paper. Draw lines up and down on the pages to look like grasses and trees. With an adult's help, make a group of tigers by cutting out tiger shapes. Put their stripes on with a marker. Cut out a few more cat shapes. Do not add stripes. These will be lions.

STEP 2 Tape your scenes to the wall. Add your tigers to one sheet. Put your lions on the other. Now ask your family and friends to be prey. Have them look at the jungles from across the room and tell you how many big cats they see. Write their answers on a chart like the one on this page.

Prey	Number of Lions	Number of Tigers
Person 1		
Person 2		
Person 3		
Person 4		
Person 5		
Totals:		

STEP 3 Add up the total number of tigers your friends and family saw. Divide this by the number of people who looked at the jungle scenes. Subtract the number of tigers they saw from the number of tigers there were. Do the same for the lions. Which cat's camouflage is best suited for the jungle?

5 Know Your FACTS

Test your knowledge of tigers.

1 How long have tigers been on Earth?

2 What genus does the tiger belong to?

3 How many species of tigers have become extinct since 1940?

4 How long do tiger cubs stay with their mother?

5 What do many Chinese people call the tiger?

ANSWERS
1 About 2 million years
2 Genus Panthera
3 Three
4 About two years
5 King of Animals

Key Words

adapted: changed to suit the environment

ancestor: a relative who lived long ago

dens: places where animals in nature rest or sleep

evolved: gradually changed over time

extinction: no longer living any place on Earth

family: a group of related animals or plants

genes: the parts of cells that carry coded information about traits passed from parent to offspring

genus: a subdivision of a family

habitats: the environments in which animals live

poachers: people who kill animals illegally

prey: an animal that is hunted for food

solitary: an animal that does not live in a family group

subspecies: a subdivision of species, typically a geographical or ecological subdivision

territory: a certain area of land used for hunting

Index

Log on to www.av2books.com

AV² by Weigl brings you media enhanced books that support active learning. Go to www.av2books.com, and enter the special code found on page 2 of this book. You will gain access to enriched and enhanced content that supplements and complements this book. Content includes video, audio, weblinks, quizzes, a slide show, and activities.

AV² Online Navigation

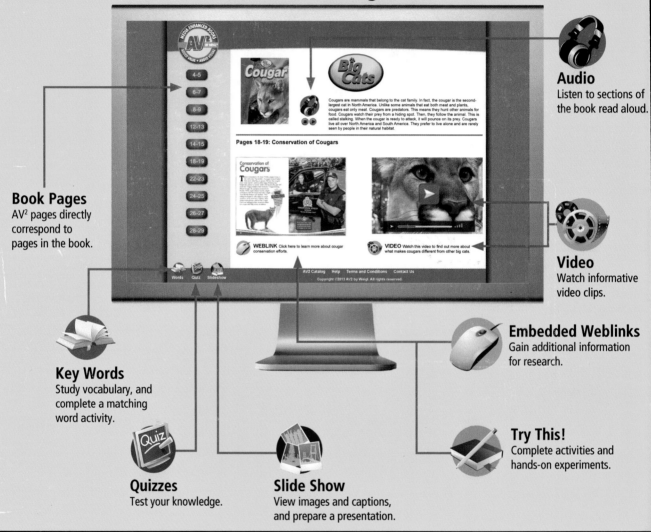

Audio
Listen to sections of the book read aloud.

Book Pages
AV² pages directly correspond to pages in the book.

Video
Watch informative video clips.

Key Words
Study vocabulary, and complete a matching word activity.

Embedded Weblinks
Gain additional information for research.

Quizzes
Test your knowledge.

Slide Show
View images and captions, and prepare a presentation.

Try This!
Complete activities and hands-on experiments.

AV² was built to bridge the gap between print and digital. We encourage you to tell us what you like and what you want to see in the future.

Sign up to be an AV² Ambassador at www.av2books.com/ambassador.

Due to the dynamic nature of the Internet, some of the URLs and activities provided as part of AV² by Weigl may have changed or ceased to exist. AV² by Weigl accepts no responsibility for any such changes. All media enhanced books are regularly monitored to update addresses and sites in a timely manner. Contact AV² by Weigl at 1-866-649-3445 or av2books@weigl.com with any questions, comments, or feedback.